GREEK
FOOD AND DRINK

Irene Tavlarios

The Bookwright Press
New York · 1988

FOOD AND DRINK

Chinese Food and Drink
French Food and Drink
Greek Food and Drink
Indian Food and Drink

Italian Food and Drink
Japanese Food and Drin
Russian Food and Drink
Spanish Food and Drink

First published in 1987 by
Wayland (Publishers) Limited
61 Western Road, Hove
East Sussex BN3 1JD, England

© Copyright 1987 Wayland (Publishers) Limited

First published in the
United States in 1988 by
The Bookwright Press
387 Park Avenue South
New York, NY 10016

ISBN 0–531–18172–3
Library of Congress Catalog Card Number 87–71049

Typeset by DP Press, Sevenoaks
Printed in Italy by G. Canale & C.S.p.A., Turin

Cover *Even though there are supermarkets in
Greece, many people still prefer to buy from small stores
like this one.*

Contents

Greece and its people

Greece is a country of dramatic scenic beauty with jagged, steep mountains and fertile, low-lying plains as well as many ancient temples, theaters and buildings, which serve as a constant reminder of its history. Located in southeast Europe, Greece is surrounded by water on three sides: the Ionian Sea to the west, the Mediterranean to the south and the Aegean to the east. Nearly a quarter of Greece is made up of islands, the largest being Crete. Around 80 percent of the land is mountainous and only 30 percent arable, a smaller proportion than in any other European country, yet over half the population is dependent on the land. The country has a population of approximately 10 million, with one in four Greeks living in or around Athens, the capital.

The frequency of war and political upheavals during ancient and modern times has meant that the Greek economy has never been consistently strong. Although industry is now increasing in importance in Greece, few industries do as well as those in other European countries. Major export

The harbor on the island of Mykonos, which is famous for its pelicans. Mykonos is just one of the many islands of Greece.

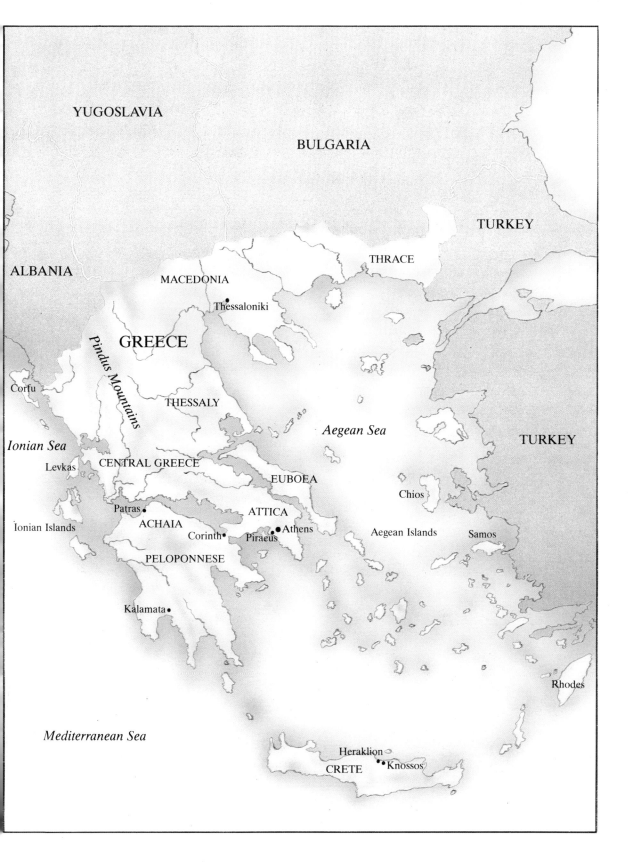

YUGOSLAVIA

BULGARIA

TURKEY

THRACE

ALBANIA

MACEDONIA

•Thessaloniki

GREECE

Pindus Mountains

Corfu

THESSALY

Aegean Sea

TURKEY

Ionian Sea

CENTRAL GREECE

Levkas

EUBOEA

Chios

Patras•

ATTICA

Ionian Islands

ACHAIA

Corinth•

•Athens

Piraeus•

Aegean Islands

Samos

PELOPONNESE

Kalamata•

Rhodes

Mediterranean Sea

Heraklion

CRETE   •Knossos

Traditional Greek dancing at festivals is an important custom.

are luxury items such as wines and tobacco.

The lack of jobs has resulted in a high rate of emigration. In the first twenty years of this century a tenth of the Greek population emigrated to the United States. Since then many have also left to settle abroad, notably in Australia and Britain. Their religion, Greek Orthodox, together with a love for their homeland, encourages the survival of Greek customs and the foods associated with them.

The Greek people differ greatly from one region to another, although they are all fiercely proud and emotional people. They combine a love of merriment with pride in their country's history, and these feelings are shown in their many festivals, which provide an opportunity to dance, sing, eat and drink!

The Greeks are a proud and emotional people who differ greatly from one region to another.

Greek food in history

In 1894, the wealthy English archaeologist, Sir Arthur Evans, set to work to excavate and reconstruct the site of the palace of Knossos on the island of Crete. He named the civilization that had flourished on the island from around 6000 B.C. until 1400 B.C., *Minoan*, after the legendary priest-king Minos. Although many things about this ancient civilization still remain unknown, archaeological finds have shown that the Minoan standard of living was very high compared to the standards elsewhere in Europe at that time.

Sir Arthur Evans's findings draw

Above   *A bust of Sir Arthur Evans, the archaeologist who excavated Knossos, a Minoan site on Crete.*

Below   *The palace of Knossos, Crete.*

a very accurate picture of Minoan foods and the way they were prepared. Giant storage jars for oil and wine, and olive and wine presses, confirm that the Minoans harvested and used the olive and the grape. Indeed, the seafaring Minoans carried on a thriving export trade in these goods. Minoan oil and wine jars have been found in lands bordering the Mediterranean as far west as Spain.

The horned sheep and short-horned cattle that graze on Crete today are similar to those raised by the Minoans and their predecessors. Meat was spit-roasted or boiled in giant bronze cauldrons, now on display at the museum at Heraklion. The shells of crabs, lobsters and other edible

Large storage jars were found in the excavations of Knossos. They are believed to have been used for wine and oil.

varieties of shellfish show that th sea was a major source of food octopus and squid appear often o pottery decorations so it is likel that they too were eaten. Bone found in a cooking pot show tha fish was boiled, and bronze fryin pans indicate that it could also hav been fried.

The grains used were barley an wheat. No ovens have been found so bread was probably cooked o hot stones and would have bee unleavened (much like *pita* bread) Other Minoan foods were leeks chickpeas, lentils, almonds, dates pomegranates, figs and honey

8

Milk was used to make cheeses and curds, as indicated by the discovery of pottery utensils for this purpose.

In 1400 B.C. Crete was invaded by the mainland Greeks, the palace at Knossos was sacked and Greece became the greatest power in the Mediterranean. However, the Minoan influence on Greek cooking was great. In the fifth century B.C. the ancient Greeks built a civilization that the world still admires today; although the fifth century ended violently with the Peloponnesian War (431–404 B.C.). **Internal disunity, the disastrous**

In the fifth century, a civilization was created which the world still admires today. The Acropolis in Athens is one of the most famous examples of architecture from this period.

effects of Greek cities at war with each other, made Greece powerless against an outside invader, Macedonia. In 338 B.C. Greece was conquered by Philip II of Macedonia, the father of Alexander the Great. It was around this time that the first known cookbook was written, by Archestratus in 350 B.C., and many recipes, such as *dolmades* (stuffed vine leaves) and *keftethes* (meatballs) are still in use.

Alexander the Great succeeded in uniting the quarrelsome Greeks by conquering a vast empire that stretched from the Mediterranean to the Indian Ocean. Alexander was very fond of vegetables and introduced many that were new to Greece, including the onion from Egypt, the haricot bean from India,

and rice from Persia. After the death of Alexander, the Greeks fell once more into disunity and were invaded and conquered by Rome in 197 B.C.

In his book "Deipnosophists" ("The Philosophy of Dining") written in A.D. 200, Athenaeus presents a picture of foods and eating customs of the Ancient Greeks revealing that the Greeks were the first people to eat oysters, and grow cabbage and artichokes, as well as create baked foods such as pastries and gingerbread.

The Roman Empire collapsed in A.D. 330. In the Middle Ages Greece was part of the Byzantine Empire. To escape their Byzantine rulers, many of the smartest Greeks, who were traditionally also the finest cooks, found their way into isolated monasteries of the Greek Orthodox

Souvlakia is a Greek specialty that the Turks adopted during their occupation of Greece from 1453 until 1827.

Church. There they created dishes for the appreciative monks. They wore the same black robes as the monks, but, to make it clear who they were, they wore tall white hats instead of black ones. To this day master chefs in the West wear tall white hats.

From the fall of Constantinople (the capital of the Byzantine Empire) to the Turks in 1453, until Greece became a free nation in 1827, Greek cooks were made to use the Turkish language when speaking of their dishes; for example, they called the Greek *souvlaki* a *shish-kebab*. This has led to the mistaken belief that such dishes were of Turkish origin.

Agriculture

Besides the lack of arable land in Greece there are also the problems of inadequate rainfall and soil erosion. The soil, although rich in minerals, is easily washed away. Many farmers in mountain areas and on the small islands are almost entirely dependent for food on what they can grow and sell locally. The development of larger, modern, irrigated farms is being encouraged. Specialized farming is carried out in Crete, the Peloponnese, the tobacco regions of Macedonia and Thrace, in the Ionian Islands and in the wine-producing regions of Levkás and Samos. Greek tobacco and cotton are equal to the best varieties in the world. Greece also exports olives, citrus fruits, fresh and dried fruits, figs, cereals, almonds, walnuts, pistachios, wines and spirits.

Crete produces mainly grapes, wines, olives, sheep and beef. The Ionian Islands lying off the west coast have a mild, Mediterranean climate and produce grains, olives, grapes and citrus fruit. The islands are particularly famous for seafood, especially lobster.

Crete, with its rugged terrain, is ideal for raising sheep.

Above *Barley is one of the main crops of the Aegean Islands. On Sifnos threshing barley is still done using traditional methods.*

The Aegean Islands produce barley, wheat, citrus fruits, grapes, and olives, but barely enough for their own needs. Fishing and sponge-diving provide a living for some people, but there is much emigration from these islands.

Macedonia and Thrace cover the rocky area in northeast Greece. In the many inland valleys the principal crop is tobacco. Vines and grains, especially wheat, are cultivated on the coastal plains.

Central Pindus is a mountainous area with good grazing for sheep and goats. In addition to livestock, the region produces cotton, citrus fruits and olives.

Most of Thessaly is a vast fertile plain and is called "the breadbasket of Greece" because the majority of

A girl selling sponges. Sponge-diving provides a living for some of the islanders in the Aegean.

12

the country's wheat is grown there, as well as fruit, cotton and olives.

Central Greece is south of Thessaly and north of the Gulf of Corinth, which separates it from the Peloponnese. Athens, the capital, and its immediate surrounding areas are rapidly becoming more and more industrialized. On the outskirts, typical Mediterranean crops such as olives, vines and wheat are cultivated.

The Peloponnese Peninsula is mostly rugged and mountainous and the land that is arable produces mainly grains and vegetables. Citrus groves along the Gulf of Corinth flank each side of the road from Corinth to Egion. Apricots, apples, cherries, peaches, quinces and nectarines are also grown. The vineyards around Pátras produce a fine range of wines which are widely exported, the most famous of these being the *Achaia Clauss*. Kalamata in the southern Peloponnese is renowned for its olives. Although not particularly large, they are considered the best flavored of all Greek olives and are exported worldwide.

Olive pickers in a grove. Olive picking is hard work since the olives have to be picked up off the ground.

Shopping for everyday meals

Greek cuisine is a healthy one – olive oil is cheap and abundant so animal fats are seldom used. Vegetables are traditionally cooked carefully and slowly without boiling so their nutritional value is preserved. Greek cooking tends to be very seasonal and relies mainly on fruit, vegetables, meat and fish of the season.

Breakfast, *proyevma*, is generally very light consisting of fresh fruit, sheep's-milk yogurt with honey, bread and cheese and coffee. Lunch, *yevma*, in rural communities is the main meal, eaten at midday,

after which schools and businesses close until the early evening and people stay at home for an afternoon rest. Supper, *deipnon*, is a light meal eaten in the late evening. City dwellers working in offices and industry tend to have a light lunch and main meal in the late evening.

In the early evening, before the meal, appetizers called *mezethes* are served (see page 18). Greeks end

Beehives on a hillside in Cephalonia. Greece is famous for its honey, which is popular eaten at breakfast mixed with yogurt.

heir meals with a simple dessert of cold fresh fruit. Cakes and sweet pastries are not eaten directly after a meal, but are enjoyed with coffee or iced water generally in the early evenings, a couple of hours before the evening meal, and on special occasions such as weddings, christenings and festival days.

With this emphasis on fresh food for each meal, shopping is very much a part of the daily routine. Even though there are super-markets in the cities, people prefer to buy from the smaller stores and the markets. Greeks always want to see, examine and choose what they are buying, and like to shop for fresh food every day. The market stands are full of color, piled high with fresh country produce: vegetables, fruits, cheeses and herbs. There are huge vats of black and green olives and a large variety of dry beans, peas, rice and other dry foods. In the meat markets, besides freshly slaughtered live-stock, there are game birds, and outside the fresh fish markets there are always the lemon sellers with their huge baskets filled with large juicy lemons to flavor the fish.

In the remote rural areas most produce is bought from street vendors. Fishmongers and green-grocers drive around in open-backed trucks (which have replaced

Vegetables and fruit at a stand on the island of Santorini, a volcanic island in the Aegean Sea.

Above *Many smaller islands, such as Ios in this picture, must have produce delivered by sea.*

Below *A mobile grocery in Cephalonia.*

he donkey and cart in most egions!) loaded with produce. hey stop in each street and call oudly to people to come and buy.

The baker, *o fournas*, and his oven re the center of daily life, articularly in the rural villages and n the islands. After the day's read is baked in the early morning, he baker's oven is used to cook neals brought in by his customers. eople who do not have adequate ooking facilities, families who all vork, as well as those who possess nodern cooking facilities but do not vish to heat up their kitchens uring the hot summers, take their repared casseroles, meats and rays of cakes in for baking and ollect them before the meal.

The *fourno* (oven) is a large beehive-shaped structure situated outdoors in a courtyard. It is filled with brushwood, which is set afire, and the opening is blocked with a metal sheet. When the flames have died down, it is raked out and after the bread has been baked, the other dishes are put in. The white wood-ash, left when the fire has gone out, was used (from ancient times up until the advent of washing machines, bleaches and detergents) for soaking linen to keep it white. This method of washing still occurs in some rural areas.

National specialties

Mezethes

Mezethes are eaten at leisure with *ouzo*, wine or other drinks either before a meal or merely as an accompaniment to the drinks. There are standard *mezethes* such as olives, cheese, anchovies and nuts, and a great variety of others depending on the season. These range from offal fried in olive oil, served with herbs and a generous squeeze of lemon, many varieties of fish (for example, sea urchins, whitebait, squid, octopus, spiny lobster and mullet), hot triangles of thin flaky *phyllo* pastry filled wit spinach and/or cheese to stuffe vine leaves, known as *dolmade Dolmades* are one of Greece's mo famous and ancient foods and ar best made with fresh young vin leaves, stuffed with meat, rice an herbs. Two other popular *mezeth* are *tzatziki*, which is a dip mad with cucumbers, strained Gree yogurt and herbs, and *taramosalat* (see recipe).

A selection of mezethes, *including, to the right of the picture,* dolmades (*stuffed vine leaves*).

Taramosalata

You will need:

3½ ounces *tarama* (gray mullet roe) or
    smoked cod roe (available in
    specialty food stores)
1 large clove garlic, crushed
½ cup olive oil
juice of 2 lemons
1 small finely grated onion (optional)
4 slices dry white bread or 2
    medium-sized boiled, floury
    potatoes
freshly ground black pepper

What to do:

(1) Soak the *tarama* in water for about 5 minutes to remove some of the salt. Squeeze out any excess moisture and, using a bowl and wooden spoon or a blender, work into a fine creamy consistency. Add the garlic. If you wish to use onion add it next and work it in well. (2) Remove the crusts from the bread and discard. Soak the bread in cold water for about 5 minutes and then squeeze out the water lightly, without leaving it too dry. (3) Add the bread and/ or potato and work in well until the consistency is smooth again. Gradually add the olive oil and lemon juice alternately until the color is very pale pink and the texture is light, fluffy and creamy. (4) Garnish with black olives and serve with fresh crusty bread or pita bread.

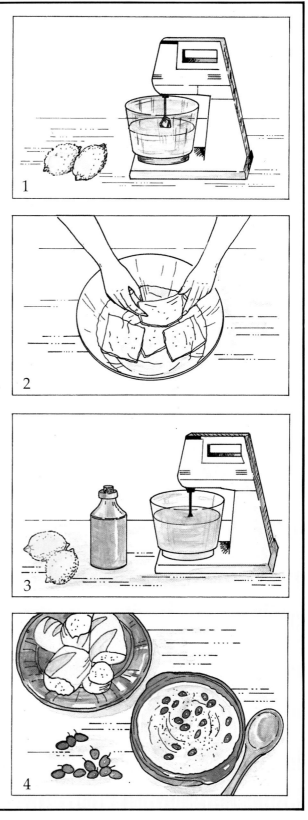

19

Taramosalata is a creamy fish roe pâté, and the basic ingredient is the salted and pressed roe of the gray mullet, although smoked cod roe can be used instead. There are many different ways of making *taramosalata* but the basic recipe method is the same.

Soups

One of the ways in which Greek culture influenced Mediterranean cooking is in the making of soup. There is little doubt that *bouillabaisse* was introduced by the Greeks in the sixth century B.C. to the Marseilla Phocaem Colonies (Marseilles) under the name of *kaccavia*. A *kaccavia* was the name of a type of earthenware pot in whic fishermen on long journeys used t cook. It was placed in the middle c their fishing boats and they woul sit around it and help themselves The name was translated into th French *bouillabaisse* from *bouillote*, o pot.

Soup very often constitutes main dish. Some are so thick an substantial that they are a meal i themselves. Bean or lentil soups ar eaten largely during Lent when th Orthodox Church disapproves c the eating of meat. In ancient time *fassolada*, a bean soup, was

Kacavia, a kind of fish soup that is popular al over Greece.

taple winter dish as it is today.

Avgolemono was referred to by Athenaeus in *Deipnosophists*, and is till the most popular soup in Greece to this very day. It is simply and quickly made from any white stock and is light, nourishing and easily digested. The beaten eggs

Avgolemono

You will need:

6 cups fish or chicken stock
½ cup long grain rice, or *vermicelli*, tapioca or any soup pasta
3 eggs
juice of two lemons
freshly ground black pepper

What to do:

(1) Bring the stock to the boil and add the rice or pasta. Cover and simmer for about 15 minutes until the rice or pasta is cooked. (2) While the soup is cooking, separate the egg whites from the yolks.

Add one teaspoon of cold water to the whites and beat until they are a frothy, stiff meringue consistency. (3) Add the egg yolks while still beating, then add the lemon juice gradually. Very slowly ladle a little of the stock into the egg and lemon continuing to beat all the time. (4) Remove the soup from the heat and gradually add the egg mixture stirring vigorously. Add pepper and serve immediately. This soup cannot be reheated once the egg and lemon mixture has been added or it will curdle.

give a creamy, frothy texture and the lemon juice gives a refreshing tang. Variations can be made by adding rice, *vermicelli* or any type of soup pasta. It is also used as a sauce for many dishes such as *dolmades*.

To make *avgolemono* sauce, use eggs and lemon juice and prepare in the same way as for the soup. Add a little liquid from the dish the sauce will be served with, remembering to beat continuously, and add the liquid very slowly so that you do not curdle the eggs. This sauce is used for *dolmades*, poached fish, chicken and veal dishes and steamed or boiled vegetables.

Fish

As the Greek mainland is practically surrounded by the sea and the rest of the country consists of hundreds of little islands, it is no surprising that fish is part of the staple diet. Particularly on the islands, the fish is bought while still alive, as people wait on the wharf for the fishing boats to come in. The favorite way of cooking fish is to grill it over charcoal, otherwise it is mixed with various vegetables particularly onions and tomatoes and either simmered very slowly o

Octopus hanging on a washing line on Ios, in the Cyclades.

baked. Fish is always served with slices of lemon, or lemon juice is used in the recipe.

In Greece, *barbouni* (red mullet) has always been an immensely popular fish. They are delicious either simply grilled (preferably over charcoal) and served with lemon wedges and salad or fried as in the recipe *barbouni tiyanito*. This is an old island recipe that fries the red mullet with a rosemary and vinegar sauce.

Psari plaki is baked fish. *Plaki* is a term meaning any fish that is braised or baked with vegetables. It is a simple healthy and nutritious dish and any type of white fish can be used, either one kind or a mixture (see recipe).

Below Barbouni tiyanito, *red mullet fried with rosemary and vinegar.*

Above *Fish is sold fresh. Here a fisherman, asleep on his gangplank, awaits customers.*

Psari plaki

You will need:
About 3 pounds fish
juice of 1 lemon
1 large sliced Spanish onion
2 crushed garlic cloves
1 tablespoon chopped dill
1 tablespoon chopped celery leaves
1 tablespoon chopped parsley
3 large beefsteak tomatoes
   (peeled if you wish)
1 teaspoon sugar
olive oil for frying

What to do:
(1) Wash the fish and pat it dry. Pour the lemon juice over the fish, season with pepper and set aside. Fry the onion until transparent. (2) Chop the tomatoes coarsely and add to the onion with the garlic, herbs and sugar. Cover and cook gently for 15 minutes. (3) Spoon some of this sauce into the base of a baking dish, add the fish then top with the remaining sauce. Cover and cook in a moderate oven for 1 hour. Remove the cover after 40 minutes, baste the fish well and continue to cook uncovered. (4) Garnish with lemon slices and serve with fresh crusty bread and a green salad. You can make many variations on this recipe by varying the vegetables. Try adding green peppers or spinach, carrots or olives or thinly sliced potatoes.

Safety note: Be careful when frying with hot oil, it can be very dangerous.

Meat

Greece is not a great meat-raising country. Aside from a few comparatively good areas for grazing land in the north, the rest of the country provides poor fodder for cattle. The most popular meat is lamb and young goat. The best meat cooking in Greece is done on a spit, much the same kind their ancestors used, turned by hand.

During the Turkish occupation, Greek freedom fighters (*Kleftai*, meaning "the hidden ones") waged determined guerrilla warfare against the Turks. To prevent their enemies from locating their mountain hideouts by the smell of their cooking, they wrapped and cooked all of their food in parchment. *Kleftiko arni* (lamb in parchment) is still a popular dish today in Greece.

Souvlakia is marinated meat (lamb or pork) on skewers (often known outside Greece as *kebabs*). *Souvla* is the Greek word for skewer or spit. A *souvla* varies in length from the long metal rod used for roasting a suckling pig or the Easter lamb, to

Kleftiko arni, *a dish invented by Greek freedom fighters, is still popular today.*

the small spits of bamboo used to spear small cubes or meat called *souvlakia*. These may be cooked in the broiler, but are best when barbecued over charcoal. They are delicious served on a bed of rice with salads and particularly when eaten outdoors!

Souvlakia

You will need:
lamb, beef, or lean pork
olive oil (about 1 tablespoon per pound of meat)
lemon juice (½ lemon per pound of meat)
oregano
freshly ground black pepper

What to do:
(1) Cut the meat into small pieces (about the size of a walnut) and thread onto the skewers. If you wish, put a small piece of onion, green pepper or a bit of bay leaf between each piece of meat. (2) Beat the lemon juice into the olive oil, season with the oregano and black pepper. Dip the *souvlakia* into the marinade for at least half an hour. (3) Cook under a very hot broiler, turning constantly, so that the meat becomes well seared on the outside and tender and juicy inside. (4) Serve immediately and garnish with lemon quarters to squeeze over the meat.

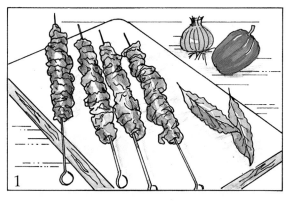

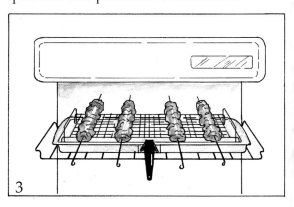

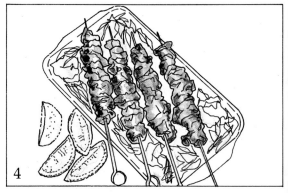

Vegetable dishes and salads

The Greeks make main dishes from a variety of vegetables, and like to eat wild vegetables as much as cultivated ones. Dandelion leaves, for example, known in Greece as *radikia*, are very popular, and several varieties are cultivated and sold in the markets, although the wild varieties are considered to be the greater delicacy. The leaves are gathered when young and tender, before they flower, and are either boiled or eaten cold with a dressing of olive oil and lemon juice, making a wonderful addition to a meal of grilled fish or meat. Other

Above   *A butcher's shop on mainland Greece. Lamb and goat are the most popular meats in Greece.*

Below   *Eggplant and tomatoes, important ingredients in many Greek specialties, are seen here on sale at a market stand.*

popular vegetables include eggplant, zucchini, broad beans, string beans, spinach, okra, peppers, artichokes, root vegetables and of course "salad vegetables." Vegetables are stuffed, boiled, fried, stewed or baked. *Bamyes*, okra or "ladies' fingers," make a delicious stew, which is equally good eaten hot or cold, on its own or with chicken or grilled lamb.

A very famous Greek vegetable dish is *spanakopita*, made with tissue-thin *phyllo* pastry and spinach, which can be served hot as a main or side dish or cold as a *meze* or appetizer.

Yemista, which literally translated means stuffed, is any variety of vegetables, such as tomatoes, peppers, eggplant or zucchini, which are stuffed with rice, herbs and meat or nuts and baked in the oven. The stuffing cooks inside the vegetable and absorbs the moisture and different flavors of its casing. The result is a colorful meal with lots of different and delicious flavors. This is one of the most frequently made meals in Greek homes.

Spanakopita *is a vegetable dish made with* phyllo *pastry and spinach.*

Stewed okra

You will need:

1 pound fresh okra
4 large peeled and chopped tomatoes
1 finely chopped medium-sized onion
1 crushed clove garlic
2 tablespoons chopped flat-leaved
  parsley
freshly ground black pepper
pinch of salt
2 tablespoons olive oil

What to do:

(1) Wash the okra well with cold water, then pat it dry with paper towels. Handling each okra pod with care, peel the outer part off the head of each one with a paring knife, taking care not to cut into the flesh and seeds, or the inner juices will leak and the dish will become glutinous when cooked. (2) Each okra pod should be intact with its juice sealed in. (3) In a frying pan sauté the onion, garlic and parsley in olive oil until the onion is clear, not browned. Add the tomatoes, stir and cook for a couple of minutes. (4) Add the okra, stir well, season, cover and simmer until tender. Okra is often added to lamb or chicken stew. Simply stir the okra into the stew (being careful not to break the okra) about 20 minutes before the stew has finished and simmer until the okra is tender.

Safety note: Take great care when taking the head off the okra with the knife, or ask an adult to do it.

29

Salads are a constant accompaniment to any Greek meal. They are made with a large choice of vegetables, including many wild varieties and herbs from the mountains, and simply dressed with olive oil and lemon or vinegar. *Diafora salata* (mixed salad) can be

A young girl in a taverna *enjoying a* horiatiki *salad made with tomatoes,* feta *cheese and olives.*

made with any combination of greens, together with tomatoes, olives, capers, cucumbers, onion, cheese, radishes, herbs and anchovy fillets. The result is a spectacular salad with a wonderful variety of color tones, textures and flavors.

One of the simplest and most popular salads is *horiatiki salata* (see recipe), which is wonderful with grilled or barbecued meat or fish.

Horiatiki salata

You will need:
3 large beefsteak tomatoes, thinly
   sliced
1 medium onion, thinly sliced
3½ ounces *feta* cheese, crumbled
1 tablespoon chopped fresh oregano
3 tablespoons olive oil
dash wine vinegar or lemon juice
freshly ground black pepper
black olives
sliver of garlic

What to do:
(1) Use the garlic to rub the inside of the salad bowl thoroughly, then discard. Put the tomato and onion slices in the bowl. (2) Sprinkle the oregano, cheese, olives and pepper on top. (Salt is not necessary, as there is enough in the *feta*). (3) Pour the olive oil evenly over the top and allow to stand at room temperature for about 20 minutes so the flavors can mingle. Sprinkle on the vinegar or lemon juice.

31

Cheeses

Most Greek cheeses are soft and are made from either ewe's or goat's milk. They are made by shepherds from very old traditional recipes. Some of the more popular varieties are now being made commercially for export to the vast Greek communities abroad, particularly in the U.S., Australia and Britain.

Feta is the most popular and well-known Greek cheese. *Feta* is white, soft, tangy, crumbly and extremely good to eat. It is made in the same way as most farmhouse cheeses milk is curdled with rennet and allowed to drain until firm (the whey is kept), then salted and packed into wooden kegs. *Feta* is made from goat's, ewe's or cow's milk and each tastes slightly different.

Myzithra is a soft, unsalted subtly flavored cheese made from the whey that is drained away during the making of *feta*, and then

Feta *cheese is added to a variety of salads.*

Cheeses in Greece are usually made from either ewe's or goat's milk.

ixed with fresh ewe's milk. It is elicious eaten with bread and oney and is used for cooking in any sweet dishes.

Gravieri is a rich, creamy cheese om Crete. It is best served with esh fruit at the end of a meal.

Kefalotyri is a hard, salty cheese ith a hard rind. It is easily grated nd used mainly as a cooking heese or sprinkled over a dish, like alian Parmesan.

Kasseri is a firm pale golden heese that is eaten fresh. It is also sed in cooking, grated over acaroni. A popular flavorful dish

called *saganaki* is made by cutting fairly thick slices of *kasseri* (*kefalotyri* can also be used), dusting them with flour, frying in a little hot olive oil until slightly browned and serving piping hot with a squeeze of lemon juice.

Kopanisti is a blue cheese with a sharp, peppery flavor. It is made in a similar way to *feta*, but the setting time is longer. The cheese is ready to eat after ripening for one or two months.

Herbs

In the fifth century B.C., Hippocrates (known as the father of medicine) used over 400 herbs in his cures and cooking, 200 of which are still in use today. Many wild herbs are gathered on the stony hillsides but not all are used in cooking. The following herbs are just a few that feature in many Greek dishes.

Rigani (oregano) grows wild on the mountains and is probably the most widely used in cooking. It is sprinkled on salads, grilled meats

Herbs such as bay, oregano and rosemary ar important ingredients in Greek cooking.

and fish.

Capari (capers) grow wild in th countryside and are gathered i autumn to be pickled in wir vinegar. They are used to garnis boiled fish, shellfish and salads.

Dendrolivano (rosemary) grow extensively in Greece and is used flavor roast lamb and various fis dishes.

Maitano (flat-leaved parsley)

grown all year round and is widely used.

Daphni (bay) has leaves that are widely used in cooking, and you will find bay of the bush or tree variety growing in most gardens. The dried leaves are sold in all grocery stores.

The spearmint variety of *thiosmos* (mint), with its darkly veined, sharp pointed leaves is widely used in meat and vegetable dishes. Mint tea is very refreshing and a safe cure for indigestion.

The nuts used in many of the country's sweet dishes can be bought from nut sellers like the one in the picture.

Candy, cake and pastry

The main ingredients of most Greek desserts, *ylika*, are nuts, spices, clear honey and *phyllo* pastry. The Greeks are so fond of sweet things that even some breads, particularly those made for festive occasions, are cakelike in taste and texture. Many Greek pastries and sweet dishes are of ancient origin. Two of the better known Greek desserts are *melopitta* and *baklava*. *Melopitta* is a honey cheesecake traditionally made with *myzithra* cheese. *Baklava* is made with layer upon layer of flaky, buttery *phyllo* pastry, spices, ground walnuts and almonds and a sweet honey sauce. It is rich, sticky and very delicious and is best made a day or two before being served (see recipe on next page).

Baklava, *which is made with* phyllo *pastry, honey and ground nuts, is one of the most famous sweet dishes.*

Baklava

You will need:
1 pound chopped walnuts
7 ounces chopped almonds
1 pound *phyllo* pastry
7 ounces unsalted butter
1 cup sugar
1 cup water
2 teaspoons powdered cinnamon
½ teaspoon of nutmeg

For the syrup:
1 cup Greek honey
1 cup sugar
1 cup water
juice of 1 lemon

(1) Heat half the butter with one cup of sugar and one cup of water. Add the chopped nuts. Line a well-buttered baking tin with three or four sheets of *phyllo*, brushing each one well with melted butter. (2) Spread a thin layer of the nut filling on the pastry, sprinkle with cinnamon and cover with two more sheets of buttered *phyllo*. Continue in this way, using alternate layers of nut mixture and *phyllo*. Tuck the ends and sides in to contain the filling. Cover the last layer of nut mixture with three or four sheets of *phyllo*, making sure that each one is liberally brushed with melted butter. (3) Brush the top with melted butter and score into diamonds or squares with a sharp knife. Bake in a moderate, preheated oven at 300°F for about an hour or until the top is golden brown and crisp. (4) To make the syrup, boil the sugar, honey, water and lemon juice and while still hot pour it over the cooked *baklava* and allow to cool.

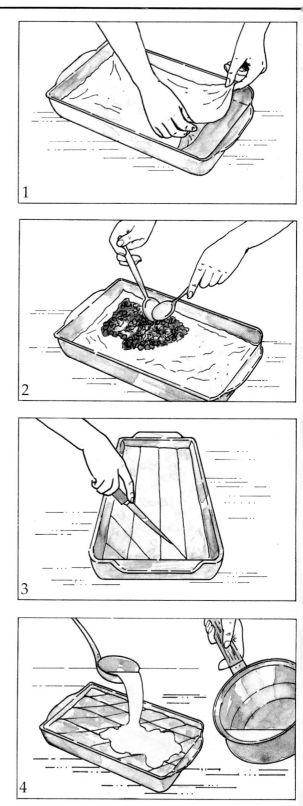

Wines, spirits and liqueurs

The Greeks have drunk wine for thousands of years. In ancient times, Dionysus, the god of wine, was worshiped and revered. Ancient Greeks would dip bread into wine and olive oil in the early morning for breakfast.

Greek wines vary enormously, mainly because the grape growers use different varieties of grapes. There are at least five hundred different varieties cultivated today.

At the time of the grape harvest, roads around the vineyards are cluttered with a constant stream of trucks, mules and donkey carts, all

Grapes growing on overhead vines are a common sight in Greece.

A mule being loaded with grapes to be taken to the presses at grape harvest time.

loaded with grapes on their way to the commercial wine presses or to the small private ones. The processing at the private presses is more of a festival in its own right than a necessary job. The grapes are loaded through an opening in the wall of the press onto the cement floor of the pressing room.

Here several men will be ready, with bare, scrubbed feet and trousers rolled up to their thighs, to tread the grapes. Some wear a carnation behind their ear, some a small bunch of grapes, and as they begin to work with skill and precision they sing songs about the grapes and the wine, their voices getting louder as the tempo of the treading rises. As the grapes are loosened from the skins, the juice flows through an opening into a vat below. As each batch is finished, the skins are swept away and the process starts again.

Holiday celebrators enjoy a bottle of Demestica *with their meal.*

Retsina is probably the most unique and distinctive Greek wine. Its origins go back to the days before bottles and casks, when wine was kept in goatskins, caulked and preserved with pine resin. Huge terracotta containers (called *amphoras* by the ancient Greeks), full of *retsina* and sealed with pitch pine resins, have been discovered intact in the bottoms of ships wrecked thousands of years ago in the Aegean and Mediterranean seas. The Greeks became accustomed to the taste and continued to add pine resin as a flavoring after both casks and bottles had been invented. There are many varieties of *retsina* produced all over the country. It comes in three basic types. Generally it is a golden wine, but there is also a rosé, *kokkinelli*, and a red, *kokkini*. The better known brands of *retsina* are *Patraiki*, *Cambas* and *Achaia Clauss*.

Some of the other well known Greek wines are *Demestica*, *Castel Danielis* and *St. Helena* (which are all produced in Achaia in the Peloponnese), *Maurodaphne* and *Nemea*. In addition, a vintage port, *grand Commandaria*, which is known as "the wine of the crusaders," is produced in Cyprus.

Greece produces a variety of brandies, which are popular worldwide.

Achaia Clauss is a liqueur brandy aged seven years from Achaia; *Cambas* is an excellent ten-year-old

From left to right, ouzo, *brandy and mastic liqueur.*

brandy from Attica and the Peloponnese; *Metaxas* is a full-bodied brandy, aged five or seven years, from Piraeus; and *Sans rival* is a five-year-old brandy from Piraeus.

Ouzo is a clear, aniseed-flavored spirit, the by-product of wine making. It can be taken alone, with water or with ice as an aperitif. Mixing with water or ice makes it cloudy and white. Village-made *ouzo* can be very strong. The Greeks rarely drink *ouzo* without eating.

Mastiha is a clear liqueur flavored with gum mastic. The island of Chios has more than four million mastic trees, which are tapped for their pale, amber-colored sap. The sap has been used since ancient times as chewing gum. Crushed gum mastic is also used to flavor breads, cakes and candies. *Mastiha* is a pleasant drink and can be taken alone or with water or ice.

Festive foods

Greeks have many ritual customs covering just about every event in life, from birth to death, as well as many religious festivals.

Easter is by far the most important event in the Greek Orthodox Church. The traditions of celebration are observed not only in the smallest villages and major cities of Greece but anywhere in the world where there is a Greek community.

No meat, fish or dairy products are eaten during Lent. Lentils and thick soups, bread made only of flour and water, and vegetabl[e] dishes are all eaten at this time. Some popular recipes like *dolmade*[s] and *yemista* are adapted for Lent b[y] using pine nuts and herbs instea[d] of meat.

The date of Easter is determine[d] by the Julian calendar. Greek Easte[r] must always follow the Jewis[h] Passover. Each day during Hol[y] Week leading up to Easter, th[e]

A Greek Orthodox wedding. Weddings are just one of the occasions for celebration and special food in Greece.

At festival time in Greece the children all dress up in costumes.

egg, someone will come toward you with an egg in hand and challenge you. You hold your egg with the pointed end up. The other person holds an egg with the pointed end down and gently taps your egg saying "Christos Anesti" (Christ is risen), and you reply "Alithos Anesti" (Truly, He is risen). One of the eggs will crack. If it is yours, you lose. If your opponent's egg cracks you win and go on to challenge someone else. Traditional red egg dye is simple to use and is imported by all countries that have Greek communities.

events of Christ's life are remembered. On Palm Sunday, for example, palm crosses are distributed and the eating of fish is permitted, as it is a happy day.

On Holy Thursday, eggs are dyed a deep red to symbolize the blood of Christ. When the red shell is removed, revealing the egg white, this symbolizes the Resurrection. A bowl of these is kept for offering to friends and visitors on Easter Sunday. These eggs are also distributed after the midnight church service on Easter Saturday night/Easter Sunday morning. When you are given an

Special Easter bread with dyed eggs.

In the mountains the sheep feed on the shoots of mountain herbs, which gives their meat a special taste at Easter.

On Saturday of Holy Week each family slaughters a lamb. Young lambs, born from January to March on the mountains, feed on the spring shoots of wild mountain herbs, which gives their meat a wonderful taste. By Easter the lambs are ready for market and thousands are herded down to the cities with their heads decorated with festive blues and pinks. In the villages, each family traditionally raises a milk-fed lamb or goat to be slaughtered and baked in the *fourno* (oven).

While the lambs are slaughtered and prepared, pinewood fires are lit in the ovens, and when the embers are red hot the meat is put in. Then the opening of the oven is sealed with clay and rocks to keep the temperature even, so that the meat cooks overnight without burning. On the next day, Easter Sunday, the ovens are opened and the feasting begins. Many people roast their Easter lamb on the Sunday morning over a pinewood fire using a hand-turned spit, which is exactly the same method their pagan ancestors used centuries ago before the advent of Christianity.

The ceremony of cutting the New

Year Cake, the *vasilopitta*, goes back to the days of the Byzantine Empire and takes place traditionally at midnight on New Year's Eve. The head of the family performs the ceremony with his whole family gathered about him. The first piece he cuts is for Christ, the second for Saint Basil, the patron saint of the Greek New Year. These are placed on one side; the third piece is for the house, the fourth for the head of the house, (usually the father or grandfather), the fifth for the mother or grandmother and each succeeding piece is cut for other members of the family in order of age, until the cake has been divided equally. Traditionally, a gold coin is baked in the cake. Whoever finds the coin in their portion will have good luck in the coming year. If the coin is found in the portion laid aside for Christ, Saint Basil or the house, it means luck for all assembled.

Kourabiethes are Greek shortbreads, which are traditionally made for Christmas. Saint John Chrysostom is said to have mentioned *kourabiethes* during one of his sermons. Each *kourabie* is topped with a whole clove to symbolize the Three Wise Men who brought gifts to the baby Jesus.

Special foods especially baked for Christmas, including kourabiethes *(bottom and left)*.

Kourabiethes

You will need:
2 pounds (7½ cups) flour
1 pound unsalted butter
¾ cup sugar
1 teaspoon baking powder
1 tablespoon brandy
1 teaspoon vanilla
2 egg yolks
rosewater (available at specialty stores)
confectioner's sugar
cloves

What to do:
(1) Sift the flour with the baking powder two or three times. Cream the butter with the sugar and then add the brandy, the vanilla and the egg yolks; add enough flour to make a soft but firm dough. (2) With your hands form the dough (about ½ a tablespoon at a time) into crescent shapes and place on a floured baking sheet. (3) Place a whole clove into each one and bake in a moderate oven at 350°F for about 20 minutes or until the cookies are cooked through but not browned. (4) Remove from the oven and sprinkle with confectioner's sugar and then rosewater while still hot. Repeat once more, then cool. In a cookie tin they will stay fresh for 2 to 3 weeks.

Safety note: Always be careful when taking anything hot out of the oven, or ask an adult to do it for you.

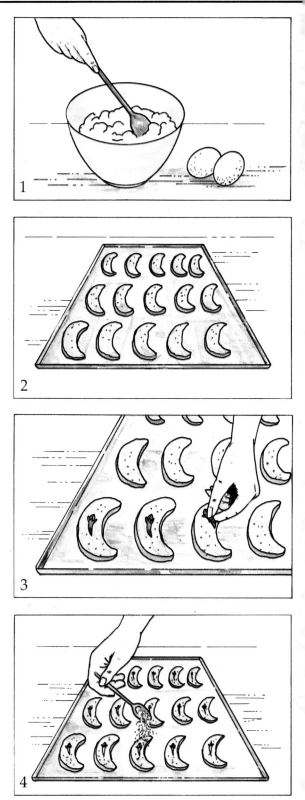

Glossary

Ancestors People very far back in one's family history.

Arable land Land fit for plowing or growing crops.

Archaeologist A person who studies objects and relics from ancient times, before man began to record history.

Avgolemono Egg-and-lemon-based sauce.

Emigration The act of leaving one's country to settle in another.

Excavate To uncover ruins by digging out.

Julian Calendar The calendar introduced by Julius Caesar in 46 B.C. It is identical to our present calendar, except that the beginning of the year was not fixed at January 1 and leap years occurred every fourth year and every centenary.

Lent The period of forty days, lasting from Ash Wednesday to Easter Saturday, observed by the Christian Church to commemorate Jesus's fasting in the wilderness.

Mastic An aromatic resin obtained from the mastic tree, a small Mediterranean evergreen.

Offal The nutritious insides of an animal, such as the heart, liver, kidneys and tongue.

Phyllo pastry Paper-thin pastry, in layers.

Pine nuts Kernels from the cones of the *Pinus Pinea*, the species of pine native to the Mediterranean.

Pita bread A flat rounded bread that is only slightly leavened. It has a hollow inside that can be stuffed with food.

Rennet An acid, taken from the stomach of a calf, that curdles milk for cheese.

Resin A natural substance that oozes out of certain trees.

Soil erosion The wearing away of soil by the action of water, ice or wind.

Tarama The roe (eggs) of the gray mullet.

Sea urchins (*achinoi*) Seafood usually served as an appetizer. The shell is pried open and the orange/yellow roe is scooped out and eaten. It is delicious eaten on its own or with a dash of lemon juice and olive oil.

Unleavened Made from dough containing no yeast.

Whey The watery part of milk that is separated from the curd (the thick part).

Greek words and phrases

General

Kalimera	Good morning/day.
Kalispera	Good evening.
Kalinikta	Good night.
Parakalo	Please.
Evkaristo	Thank you.
Adio	Goodbye.

Ti ora enai, parakalo?
What time is it, please?

Pou enai . . . ?
astinomia/yiatros/telephono/estiatorio/
agora/xenothochio
Where is . . . ?
the police station/doctor/
telephone/restaurant/market/
hotel

To onoma mou enai . . .
My name is . . .

At the restaurant

Psomi	Bread
Voutyro	Butter
Tyri	Cheese
Salata	Salad
Mezethes	Appetizers
Psari	Fish
Arni	Lamb
Kreas	Meat
Kotopoulo	Chicken
Patates	Potatoes
Soupa	Soup
Gala	Milk
Krasi	Wine
Nero	Water
Psito	Roast
Tiganito	Fried
Frouta	Fruit
Payoto	Ice cream
Yliko	Sweet

Ena trapezi yia tessera atoma,
parakalo
A table for four people, please.

To logariasmo, parakalo
The bill, please.

Further reading

Betty Crocker's Cookbook for Boys and Girls. Western Publishers, 1984.

Cooking the Greek Way by Lynne W. Villios. Lerner Publications, 1984.

The Fannie Farmer Junior Cookbook by Wilma L. Perkins. Little, 1957.

Follow the Sun: International Cookbook for Young People by Mary Deming and Joyce Haddard. Sun Scope, 1982.

Greek Everyday Life by Roger and Sarah Nichols. Longman, 1978.

Let's Look Up Food from Many Lands by Beverly Birch. Silver, 1985.

Take a Trip to Greece by Keith Lye. Franklin Watts, 1983.

Picture Acknowledgments

The publishers would like to thank the following for their persmission to reproduce copyright pictures: Anthony Blake 10, 20, 23 (bottom), 25, 28, 33, 34, 35 (right), 39, 43; Cephas Picture Library 8, 12 (top), 14, 15, 16, 22, 27 (bottom), 42; Greg Evans Photo Library 6 (bottom), 11, 12 (bottom), 30, 32, 37 (top), 38; Andrew Hasson 41 (top); Hutchison Library 4, 6 (top), 17, 35 (left), 37 (bottom), 40; Ronald Sheridan Photo Library 7 (top); Wayland Picture Library 7 (bottom), 13; ZEFA 9, 18, 23 (top), 27 (top), 41 (bottom). The map on page 5 is by Malcolm Walker. All step-by-step illustrations are by Juliette Nicholson.

Index